AL-GHAZZALI
ON HOPE AND FEAR

Ḥujjat al-Islām Abū Ḥāmid
Muḥammad Ghazzālī Ṭūsī

TRANSLATED FROM THE PERSIAN BY
MUHAMMAD NUR ABDUS SALAM

INTRODUCTION BY
LALEH BAKHTIAR

SERIES EDITOR
SEYYED HOSSEIN NASR

GREAT BOOKS OF THE ISLAMIC WORLD

Library of Congress Cataloging-in-Publication Data

Ḥujjat al-Islām Abū Ḥāmid Muḥammad Ghazzālī Ṭūsī (AH450/CE1059 to AH505/CE1111), commonly known as al-Ghazzali. *Al-Ghazzali On Hope and Fear* from the *Alchemy of Happiness (Kimiya al-saadat)*, the Persian translation by al-Ghazzali of the *Ihya ulum al-din (Revival of the Religious Sciences)*
1. Islamic psychology. 2. Sufism. 3. Islamic theology—Early works to 1800. 4. Ghazzali, 1058-1111. I. Title.

ISBN: 1-57644-706-6 pbk

Cover design: Liaquat Ali
Cornerstones are Allah and Muhammad connected by *Bismillāh al-Raḥmān al-Raḥīm* (In the Name of God, the Merciful, the Compassionate).

Logo design by Mani Ardalan Farhadi
The cypress tree bending with the wind, the source for the paisley design, is a symbol of the perfect Muslim, who, as the tree, bends with the wind of God's Will.

Published by
Great Books of the Islamic World, Inc.
Distributed by
KAZI Publications, Inc.
3023 W. Belmont Avenue
Chicago IL 60618
Tel: 773-267-7001; FAX: 773-267-7002
email: info@kazi.org /www.kazi.org

INTRODUCTION

*". . . be not like those who forgot God and [eventually] God
caused them to forget their 'self'. . . "* (Q. 59:18-19)

There is nothing more timely today than a translation of
the remarkable work on Islam of al-Ghazzali for two
reasons. First of all, the results of recent studies of med-
icine-psychology and religious belief[1] confirm that the religious model works in the healing process so traditional wisdom must be made available in English for all researchers as
well as readers to be able to access it and draw upon it for
areas of further research. Secondly, at a time when the world
is confused by the varying beliefs of Muslims and are inter-
ested in studying what the majority of the world's Muslims
believe, the works of al-Ghazzali provide the perfect opportunity.

Abu Hamid Muhammad al-Ghazzali was born in the city
of Tus, northwestern Iran, in AD 1058.[2] He studied in Tus
until he was twenty-seven when he moved to Baghdad. He
was appointed as a professor at the Nizamiyyah college there
when he was thirty-three. After four years of a strenuous
schedule, he underwent a spiritual experience which con-
vinced him that all of the knowledge he had gained was useless in comparison to gnosis or experiential knowledge of the
Divine Presence. He realized unless he left his position and
was free to search for this knowledge deeper within himself

without worldly distractions, he would never attain it. He therefore provided for his family and left for Damascus and other well known cities at that time.

When he was forty-eight he returned to his birthplace where he lived for the next five years until his early death at the age of fifty-three.[3] He left behind over 400 works among them being his famous *Revival of the Religious Sciences* (*Ihya ulum al-din*) which he wrote in Arabic. Over 2300 pages, it is a compendium of Islamic practices. A few years after he finished the *Revival*, he felt the need to write the same sort of compendium on being a Muslim in Persian. This is the entire work here translated into English for the first time which al-Ghazzali called the *Alchemy of Happiness*. It is a masterful textbook on traditional psychology.[4]

While modern Western psychology focuses on describing emotions, behavior or cognition, that is, what we feel, do and think without recourse to the basic principles or causes, traditional psychology is based on the same three centers, but like all traditional sciences, includes much more. As a result of including metaphysics, theology, cosmology and the natural sciences as the basis or underlying principles for what we feel, do or think, it becomes a wholistic psychology. The goal of traditional psychology is to assume the noble character traits, to overcome our ego which competes for our attention with our God-given instinct to attend to the One God. In this view, there cannot be two wills and therefore our free will has to be disciplined to submit to God's will (*islam*).

The word psychology comes from the Greek words "psyche" or "soul" and "logos." Psyche also means breath, spirit and refers to the animating principle of the universe. Logos means "word" and in the traditional view it refers to "the Word of God." The science of psychology, then, when it is true to its name, is the study of the Word of God within the human soul or spirit.

Al-Ghazzali's psychology is essentially that of monotheism and unity, the world view that "there is no god, but God" or "there is no deity, but God." It is to see the universe and all that is in it as aspects of the One God. The world view of monotheism (*tawhid*) forms the underlying basis for traditional psychology.

By the word "tradition" we mean *al-din* which has been defined as: "truths or principles of a Divine Origin revealed or unveiled to mankind through a messenger along with the ramifications and application of these principles in different realms including law, social structure, art, symbols, the sciences and embracing Supreme Knowledge along with the means for its attainment."[5]

Tradition (*al-din*) is a point which is at one and the same time the Center and Origin of our being. Traditional psychology is oriented towards helping the individual as well as the human community find that Center as we prepare for the return to our Origin.

A monotheist (*hanif*) like al-Ghazzali regards the whole universe as a unity, as a single form, a single living and conscious thing, possessing will, intelligence, feeling, and purpose, revolving in a just and orderly system in which there is no discrimination no matter what one's gender, color, race, class, or faith be. All comes from God and returns to God, while a multitheist (*mushrik*) views the universe as a discordant assemblage full of disunity, contradiction, and heterogeneity containing many independent and conflicting poles, unconnected desires, customs, purposes, wills, sexes, sects, colors, races, classes, and faiths.

The monotheistic world view sees the universal unity in existence, a unity of three separate relationships: (1) our relationship with others, nature and the universe; (2) our relationship with God; (3) our relationship with our "self." These relationships are not alien to one another; there are no bound-

aries between them. They move in the same direction. Al-
Ghazzali expresses this when he writes:

> Then know that there is a station in gnosis
> (*marifat*) where, when a person reaches it, he real-
> ly sees that all that exists is interconnectedness,
> one with another, and all are like one animate
> being. The relationship of the parts of the world
> such as the heavens, the earth, the stars to each
> other is like the relationship of the parts of one ani-
> mate being to each other. The relationship of all the
> world to its Director—from one aspect, not from all
> aspects—is like the relationship of the kingdom of
> the body of an animal to the spirit and intellect
> which are its Director. Until a person recognizes
> this, that Verily, God created Adam in His image, it
> cannot be comprehended by his understanding."[6]

Other non-monotheistic religious world views see the
Divinity—or even the plural of this—as existing in a special,
metaphysical world of the gods, a higher world as contrasted
with the lower world of nature and matter. They teach that
God is separate from the world, created it and then left it
alone. In the monotheistic world view, God has never left and
is the destination of the Return. In this view, our "self" fears
only one Power and is answerable to only one Judge; turns to
one direction (*qiblah*), orienting all hopes and desires to only
one Source. A belief in monotheism gives us a sense of inde-
pendence and liberation from everything other than God and
a connectedness to the universe and all that it contains.
Submission to God's Will alone liberates us from worshipping
anything other than God and rebelling against anything else
that purports to be God.

AL-GHAZZALI'S THREE FUNDAMENTALS

Al-Ghazzali sees the basis for traditional psychology lead-
ing to self-development as consisting of three fundamentals—
the same three fundamentals confirmed by modern psychology and scientific studies—affect, behavior and cognition (the
ABC of psychology). The first fundamental is knowledge (cognition, awareness or consciousness). The second he calls states
(affect or emotion) that that knowledge or awareness produces
in us. The third he calls act or deed— the action that results
from our emotion that came from our knowledge or awareness
of something.

THE FIRST FUNDAMENTAL: KNOWLEDGE
(COGNITION)

According to al-Ghazzali, knowledge should be used to
come to understand the articles of belief rather than accepting
them on faith alone. The articles of belief include: the belief
that God is One; the belief that God sent Prophets to guide
mankind to Him and that Muhammad (ﷺ) is the Messenger
and last Prophet who will be sent (until the end of time when
Jesus (ﷺ) will return) and that the Quran is the last revelation; the belief in angels and the Scriptures; and the belief
that after death we will be resurrected in the Hereafter and
judged by God who will reward or punish us depending upon
our intentions. Al-Ghazzali says: "It is the states of the heart,
the place of our intentions, that holds us accountable."[7]

BELIEFS

Our beliefs are the guiding principles that give meaning
and direction to our life. They filter our perceptions of the
world. When we freely choose to believe something is true, a
command is delivered to our spiritual heart (mind) telling us
how to represent what we have come to believe to be true.
When the process has been accomplished with Divine Grace

(defined by al-Ghazzali as: the harmony, agreement and con-
cord of our will and action with God's will), our beliefs can
become our most effective force for creating the positive and
good in our lives. In explaining the importance of coming to the realization
of the Oneness of God oneself and not accepting it because
someone has told us, al-Ghazzali says:

> Know that the first duty incumbent upon who-
> ever becomes a Muslim is to know and believe the
> meaning of the utterance "there is no god but God,
> Muhammad is the Messenger of God," which he
> pronounces with his tongue, understands in his
> heart, and believes so that he entertains no doubt
> about it. When he has believed and his heart is
> established firmly upon (that belief)—so that doubt
> cannot touch it—it is sufficient for the basis of being
> (one who submits to God's Will (*muslim*)). Knowing
> it with evidence and proof is an individual duty
> incumbent upon every (one who submits to God's
> Will (*muslim*)). The Prophet (ﷺ) did not command
> the Arabs to seek proofs, to study theology, or to
> look for doubts and replies to those; rather, he was
> content with belief and faith.[8]

He then defines what belief in submission to God's Will
(*islam*) means:

> Know that you have been created and that you
> have a Creator Who is the Creator of all the uni-
> verse and all that it contains. He is One. He has no
> partner nor associate. He is Unique, for He has no
> peer. He always was; His existence has no begin-
> ning. He always shall be; there is no end to His exis-
> tence. His existence in eternity and infinity is a nec-
> essary, for annihilation cannot touch Him. His exis-
> tence is by His own essence. He needs nothing but

nothing is unneedful of Him. Rather, He is established by His Own essence, and everything else is
established through Him.[9]

Al-Ghazzali mentions five sources for our beliefs:
(1) Our environment: how we grow up; models of success
or failure we learn from; what is right and what is wrong;
what is possible and what is impossible.
(2) Our experiences and events as we grow up.
(3) Knowledge: what we know and do not know; that we
continue to educate our "self" from "the cradle to the grave."
(4) Results we have seen achieved in the past, learned
from the stories of past people in the Quran.
(5) Setting new goals to achieve future results.

Future results depend upon how we incorporate our
beliefs—how we view the world—into our own self image.
According to al-Ghazzali, our firm and certain belief in the
Oneness of God should lead us—as it did Prophet Muhammad
(ﷺ)—to the following beliefs:

(i) The belief that everything happens for a reason. We
look for the good and positive in whatever happens.

(ii) The belief that there is no such thing as failure, only
results or outcomes. If we are able to train a falcon to hunt for
us, al-Ghazzali uses as an example, we can train and discipline our rational faculty to control our passions. Al-Ghazzali
says that we should not expect immediate results. Change is
gradual. We need to develop patience, a great virtue in his
view.

(iii) The belief that we must take responsibility for whatever happens. No matter what happens, know and believe
that we are in charge. The Prophet never blamed others for
whatever happened. He never allowed himself to be a victim.
As the Quran says: *"God does not change the condition of a
people until they change what is within themselves."* (Q. 13:11)

(iv) The belief that we need to learn from other people who

are our greatest resource. Treat them with respect and dignity as the Prophet did.

(v) The belief that we need to challenge our profession or
line of work and excel in it. Explore new ways of doing things.
Increase our sense of curiosity and vitality.

(vi) The belief that there is no success without commitment. Know our outcome in the Hereafter as the Prophet
knew. Develop our sensory responses so we know what we are
getting and then continue to refine it until we get what we
want. Study the key beliefs of the Prophet and then hold tight
to them.

In al-Ghazzali's view, if we firmly believe we are among
those "who submit to God's Will" (*muslim*), then with our cognition, affect and behavior as understood from the monotheistic point of view as our foundation, we can submit in everything that we say or do. What we believe to be true becomes
possible when we know what we want—to be one who submits
to God's will—and believe we can achieve it.

Strategies

Developing a strategy is to duplicate our belief system.
When we organize the way we think, the way we feel and the
way we behave according to our belief system, we have developed a strategy. The ingredients of our strategy are our
human experiences. Our experiences are fed from our five
outer senses: seeing, smelling, hearing, tasting and touching.
Our five senses motivate us to action. When we are aware of
what they perceive and keep their perceptions in line with our
belief system, we have developed a successful strategy.

The amounts we use of the information provided by our
senses is monitored by our spiritual heart (mind). Are the
images small or large, bright or unclear, close up or far away?
How we put these together, their order and sequence clarifies

our strategy.

With our resource being our "self" consisting of body, spirit, soul and spiritual heart (it is our spiritual heart that centers us), we want to learn what we need to do to organize this
resource. How can we have our goal and belief achieve the
greatest potential? What is the most effective way to use the
resource of our "self" and its subparts? The most effective
strategy has always been modeling the behavior of others who
have the same goal and the same belief. For the believer, this
model is that of the Messenger Muhammad (ﷺ) who was the
perfect human being.

Strategies he used included performing the prescribed fast
as well as formal prayer, supplication and continuous recitation of the revelation. For the believer, revelation brought both
a Law and a Way. Both serve as strategies of how to approach
life in the manner in which the model approached life, and
knowing that our model did not always do things exactly the
same way.

The strategy of Quranic recitation is yet another form of
discipline. One of the verses of the Quran: *"Remember Me and
I will remember you,"* (Q. 2:152) makes this form of supplication a very rich traditional strategy to attain spiritual energy.

THE SECOND FUNDAMENTAL: STATES
(AFFECT, EMOTION)

Our belief establishes states (emotions, affect) which then
result in our actions. In this relationship and all others, our
state of mind is
important because that determines our emotion and our emotion determines how many resources are available to us. Our
emotions depend upon how we feel physically—our breathing,
posture, etc.— and how we represent the world to ourselves
internally. When we have cleared our spiritual heart of

hypocrisy in our acts of worship, our actions are to worship God and we are at the beginning stages of the greater struggle according to al-Ghazzali.

States (affect, emotion) are held or transformed in terms of psychology through moral values that energize us. Our behavior is the result of the state we are in at the time. Our emotional state governors our behavior. Behavior is the result of how we represent the information from our senses internally as well as our muscular tension, posture, physiology.

We have the resources we need to succeed. We have to learn how to access them. We need to learn to take direct control: Once we learn to manage our states (emotions), according to al-Ghazzali, we can modify our behavior. There is a difference of how people react to the same state. The difference depends on their model.

One of the best methods which al-Ghazzali uses over and over again in the *Alchemy* is that of what is today called reframing: changing the way we evaluate what something means. If our culture teaches us that change is a failure of opportunity for learning, we need to become resourceful, to realize that nothing has power over us but the power we give it by our own conscious thoughts. The meaning of any experience depends on the frame we put around it. If we change the context or reference point, the process changes.

We can reframe by context reframing or content reframing. With context reframing, we take a bad experience and show it in another way. With content reframing, we drastically change how we see, hear, or represent a situation. We learn to change the way we represent a situation so we feel differently about it. Now we are at the level of choice instead of reaction. By learning to reframe, we change our emotions so that they empower us. We can either associate or disassociate. If we associate consciously, we learn to change the way we represent things, thereby changing our behavior. We have to aim for congruence between our spiritual heart (mind) and body.

CLARITY OF MORAL VALUES

Clarity of values gives us a sense of who we are and why we do what we do. If we have an internal conflict between our values and our strategy, we will not succeed. Values determine what really matters in life. They provide us with a basis from which to make sound judgments about what makes life worth living.

Al-Ghazzali refers to verses 23:1-10 of the Quran as an example of believers who have succeeded by incorporating Quranic values:

> Certainly will the believers have succeeded: They who during their prayer humbly submissive; those who turn away from ill speech; they who are observant of the poor-due; they who guard their private parts except from their wives and those their right hands possess for indeed, they will not be blamed, but whatever seeks beyond that, then they are the transgressors; and they who are to their trusts and their promises attentive; and they who carefully maintain their prayers. Those are the inheritors. (Q. 23:1-10)

Al-Ghazzali then summarizes the verses to describe a person of good character.

> A person of good character is he who is modest, says little, causes little trouble, speaks the truth, seeks the good, worships much, has few faults, meddles little, desires the good for all, and does good works for all. He is compassionate, dignified, measured, patient, content, grateful, sympathetic, friendly, abstinent, and not greedy. He does not use foul language, nor does he exhibit haste, nor does he harbor hatred in his heart. He is not envious. He

> is candid, well-spoken, and his friendship and
> enmity, his anger and his pleasure are for the sake
> of God Most High and nothing more.[10]

In the *Alchemy* (as well as in the *Revival*), al-Ghazzali
devotes the major part of the work to clarity of moral values
by describing in great detail what he calls the Destroyers and
the Deliverers. He not only describes them in each of those
parts, but offers treatment as to how to get rid of them (the
Destroyers) or how to incorporate them into our personality
(the Deliverers). Doing this clarifies the moral values of the
one who submits to God's Will.

As a result of the performance of the acts of worship, if
accompanied by Divine Grace, the one who submits to the Will
of God will be receptive to the adoption of positive dispositions
(the deliverers) like temperance, courage, wisdom, and justice
and be able to avoid negative dispositions (the destroyers) like
anger, fear of other than God, cowardice, lust, envy, apathy,
preconsciousness (knowing that you do not know), uncon-
sciousness (not knowing that you do not know) and overcon-
sciousness (knowing but deceiving the self about it), but only
on the condition that others benefit from the positive dispositions one has attained. This, then, makes it encumbent on the
one who has submitted to the Will of God to come to know and
act upon the commands that underlie the relationship of self
to others.

ENERGY

The entire human organism is a complete system that
makes use of energy transformed from food and air to satisfy
its various natural dispositions. Perception (external and
internal senses) and motivation develop, according to traditional psychology, from the animal soul. Motivation is the seat
of impulses towards inclinations which are imprinted on the

external or internal senses and then, through filtering into what is called the practical intellect (the mind), a response is given. Three energy sources are active in this perspective: natural (venial, *tabiiya*), vital (arterial, *nafsaniyah*), and nervous (*hawaniyah*). These transformed energies are distributed throughout the body. The heart is considered to be the point of contact between the energy of the body and that of the self.

Without the necessary energy, which according to al-Ghazzali comes from spiritual practices, we reach a state of hoplessness and despair. For instance, if someone asked: "If one has been condemned to hardship, what is the benefit of the greater struggle?" Al-Ghazzali explains this attitude:

> Your question is valid. These words are correct in that they are the cause of the illness of our heart. That is, when a sign of a concept that a person has been condemned to hardship falls upon his heart, they cause him to make no effort, neither sowing nor reaping. Such a sign would be when a person who has been condemned to death becomes hungry the thought occurs in his heart not to eat. He says: "What good is bread to me?" He does not extend his hand to eat and he does not eat until by necessity he dies. If he has been condemned to poverty, he says: "Of what use is sowing seed?" so he neither sows nor reaps. And he for whom happiness has been decreed, he has been made aware that wealth and life have been decreed for him. They have been decreed because he has cultivated, done business, and consumed. Therefore, this decree is not invalid; rather it has reasons"[11]

THE THIRD FUNDAMENTAL: ACTIONS
(BEHAVIOR)

Knowledge alone is not sufficient for we who accepted the trusteeship of nature and were endowed with the Divine

Spirit which includes our abilities to choose, to discern, and to
gain consciousness of our "self." It is through actions based on
knowledge that the centered self benefits another as proof of
being centered. The major pillars include ritual purity
(*taharah*) and ritual prayer (*salah*), ritual fast (*saum*), the
paying of the alms tax (*zakah*), the pilgrimage (*hajj*), counseling to positive dispositions and preventing the development of
negative ones (*amr bil maruf wa nahy an al-munkar*) and
jihad or struggle in the Way of God, the greater struggle of
which is the inward struggle of the self (*jihad al-akbar*). The
last two are the major concern of traditional psychology.

BONDING POWER OR RAPPORT

Bonding and communicating are aspects of action—proof
of the extent of transformation through attaining the goal that
we had intended. The power to bond with others is an extra-
ordinary human power. It comes in the true sense when bonding develops from the heart and not from either the intellect
or the passions. It comes from a deep love for one's fellow
human being and arises when we try to meet the needs of others before our own needs, much like a mother with her new
born child.

Al-Ghazzali quoting from the Quran, the Prophet and the
Companions mentions how important it is to eat with other
people and to perform the formal obligatory prayer with other
people.

COMMUNICATORS

Believers should conceivably be master communicators on
all three levels—with self, with others and with the Source.
How we communicate determines the quality of our lives.
Through spiritual disciplines like, for example, prescribed
fasting, believers are given an opportunity, a challenge. If they

are able to communicate that challenge to themselves successfully, they will find the ability to change. This is not to accept prescribed fasting as only a religious duty but rather as a divine challenge, as a chance for growth instead of an experience which limits self. In this way we will become master communicators because our very life will communicate our vision, goal and beliefs to others to help them change for the better, as well.

RELATIONSHIP TO OTHERS

Al-Ghazzali discusses knowledge (cognition), states (affect) and action (behavior) in three relationships: our relationship with others; our relationship with our Creator-Guide; and our relationship with our "self."

The model for this is the *sunnah* of Muhammad (ﷺ) who said, "I was sent to complete the noble qualities of dispositions," explaining that God loves the positive dispositions and not the negative ones. Al-Ghazzali also quotes another Tradition in this regard, "By Him in whose hand is my life, no one shall enter paradise except the one who has positive dispositions." Al-Ghazzali says, "God taught [Muhammad (ﷺ)] all the fine qualities of disposition, praiseworthy paths, reports about the first and last affairs, and matters through which one achieves salvation and reward in future life and happiness and reward in the world to come."

Quoting the Traditions, al-Ghazzali shows the relationship established by the Prophet with others.

> And the Messenger (ﷺ) said: "There are not two persons who love each other for the sake of God that the one most beloved by God is the one loves the other the most." And he (ﷺ) said: "God Most High says: 'My love is a right for those who visit one another for My sake, who love each other for My

sake, who are generous to each other with their
wealth for My sake, and who aid each other for My
sake.'" And he (ﷺ) said: "On the Day of
Resurrection God Most High will say: 'Where are
those persons who loved each other for My sake so
that I may keep them in My shadow on this day
when there is no shade for the people in which to
take refuge?'" And he (ﷺ) said: "There are seven
persons on the Day of Resurrection who, when
there will be no shade for anyone, will be in the
shadow of God Most High: the just leader (imam),
the young person who began worshipping God Most
High at the beginning of his youth, the man who
leaves the mosque with his heart attached to the
mosque until he returns to it again, two people who
love each other for the sake of God Most High and
who come together for that and separate for that,
the person who remembers God Most High in private and whose eyes fill with tears, and the man
who when called by a magnificent and beautiful
woman says to her: 'I fear God Most High,' and the
man who gives voluntary charity with his right
hand so that the left hand has knowledge of it." And
he (ﷺ) said: "No one visits a brother for the sake of
God Most High save that an angel cries out, saying:
'Be happy and blessed! Thine is the heaven of God
Most High!'"

And he (ﷺ) said: "A man was going to visit a
friend. God Most High sent an angel in his path
who asked: 'Where are you going?' He replied: 'To
visit such-and-such a brother.' (The angel) asked:
'Do you have some business with him?' He said:
'No.' (The angel) asked: 'Are you related to him in
some way?' He said: 'No.' (The angel) asked: 'Has he
done something good for you?' He answered: 'No.'
(The angel) said: 'Then why are you going to him?'
He answered: 'I love him for the sake of God.' (The
angel) said: 'Then, God Most High has sent me to
you to give you the good news that God Most High

loves you because of your love for him, and has made heaven an obligation for both of you yourselves.'" And the Messenger (ﷺ) said: "The strongest resort of faith is love and enmity for the sake of God Most High."[12]

Al-Ghazzali describes relationships with others ranking them in degrees.

The first degree is that you love someone for some reason linked with him, but that motive is religious and for the sake of God Most High; as you like your teacher because he teaches you knowledge. That friendship is of a divine nature since your aim for (acquiring) this knowledge is the Hereafter, not rank or wealth. If the object be the world, that friendship is not of that kind. If you love your student so that he learn from you and may obtain the pleasure of God Most High through learning, (you) too obtain the spiritual reward of teaching. This is for the sake of God Most High. But if you love (him) for the sake of dignity and retinue, it will not be of that kind. If a person gives voluntary charity and likes a person on the condition that he deliver that to the poor; or he invites some poor people and likes a person who prepares a good meal, then such friendship is for the sake of God. Indeed, if one likes someone and gives him bread and clothing to give him the leisure to worship (God), it is friendship for the sake of God, since his motive is the peace of mind for worship.

Many religious scholars and worshippers have had friendships with the rich and powerful for this reason. Both were counted as friends for the sake of God Most High. Moreover, if one loves his own wife because she keeps him from corruption and because of the bringing forth of children who will supplicate for him, such love is for the sake of God Most High and everything you spent for her is a voluntary charity. Indeed, if one loves his student for two reasons: one that he serves him and the other that he gives him the peace of mind to perform his worship, that part which is for worship is counted as love for the sake of God most High and there is spiritual reward for it.

The second degree is greater. It is that one love a person for the sake of God without having any expectations from him; instead, it is by reason of obedience to God and for the love of Him that he loves the other. Moreover, because he is a servant of God and created by Him—such friendship is divine. It is greater because this arises from the excess of one's love of God Most High, so much so that it reaches the boundaries of passionate love. Whoever is in love with someone, loves (that person's) district and neighborhood. He loves the walls of (that person's) house; indeed, he loves the dog roaming the quarter's streets, and he likes that dog more than other (dogs). He is compelled to love the friend of his beloved, and beloved of his beloved, the people who obey the commands of his beloved; (the beloved's) servants, captives, or relatives; all of these he loves out of necessity, for his love spreads to whatever has a relation with his beloved. As his love increases so it does with the others who follow and are connected with the beloved.[13]

ESTABLISHING THE RELATIONSHIP
BETWEEN THE SELF AND OUR CREATOR-GUIDE

This relationship is established, according to al-Ghazzali, through the commands of worship (*ibadah*), which are the most fundamental means of communication between our "self" and God. They embody the same three aspects: knowledge (cognition), states (affect, process) and action (behavior). One who submits to the Will of God seeks knowledge of particular guidance. This produces a "state" (emotion) in the self which then responds with an action as al-Ghazzali explains:

> Know that object and kernel of all acts of worship are the remembrance of God Most High; that the buttress of Islam is obligatory formal prayer, the object of which is the remembrance of God Most High. As He said: *Surely (formal) prayer prevents lewdness and evil, and indeed the remembrance of God is greater (than all else).* (Q. 29:45)
>
> Reading the Quran is the most meritorious of the acts of worship, for the reason that it is the word of God Most High: (reading or reciting it) is remembering Him. Everything that is in it all cause a renewal of the remembrance of God, may He be praised and exalted. The object of fasting is the reduction of the carnal appetite so that the heart, liberated from the annoyance of the carnal appetites, becomes purified and the abode of remembrance; for when the heart is filled with carnal appetite, it is not possible to remember (Him); nor does (the remembrance) affect one. The object of the greater pilgrimage, which is a visit to the House of God, is the remembrance of the Lord of that House and the incitement of longing for meeting Him.
>
> Thus the inner mystery and the kernel of all of the acts of worship are remembrance. Indeed, the basis of Islam is the declaration: "there is no god but God"; this is the source of remembrance. All other acts of worship stress this remembrance. God's remembrance of you is the fruit of your remembrance of Him; what fruit could be greater than this? For this He said: *So remember Me, I shall remember you.* (Q. 2:152)
>
> This remembrance must be continuous. If it is not continuous, it should be most of the time; for salvation is tied to it. For this He said: *And remem-*

ber God much; perhaps you will be successful. (Q.
62:10) He says that if you have the hope of salvation, the key to that is much remembrance, not a little, and more frequently, not less.

And for this He said: *Those who remember God
standing, sitting, and lying down.* (Q. 3:191) He
praised these people because they do not neglect
(remembrance) standing, sitting, lying down, or in
any condition. And He said: *Remember thy Lord, (O
Muhammad), within thyself humbly and with awe,
in a soft voice, in the morning and in the evening,
and be not of the neglectful.* (Q. 7:205) He said:
*"Remember Him with weeping, fear, and in conceal-
ment, morning and evening, and do not neglect
(this) at any time."*

The Messenger (ﷺ) was asked: "What is the
best of acts?" He answered: "That you die with your
tongue moist with the remembrance of God Most
High." And he said: "Should I not inform you of the
best of your actions—the most acceptable to the
King, may He be exalted—and your highest
degrees, that which is better than giving alms of sil-
ver and gold, and better than shedding your blood
in battle against enemies in defense of the faith?"
They asked: "What is that, O Messenger of God?"
He said: "The remembrance of God." The remembrance of God Most High! And he said: "Whoever
remembering me engages in worshipful supplication of God, his gift is, in my opinion, greater and
better than giving (charity) to beggars." And he
said: "The remember of God Most High among the
heedless is like a living person amongst the dead, or
like a green tree amongst dead vegetation, or like
the warrior for the faith who stands fighting
amongst those fleeing. . .[14] In summary, the
strength of one's love for God Most High is in accor-
dance with the strength of one's faith. The stronger
one's faith, the more overwhelming one's love is.[15]

KNOW YOUR "SELF"

The most important relationship for the purposes of traditional psychology is that of our relationship to our "self." Our "self" as we have seen, consists of body, spirit, soul and spiritual heart. We turn now to the *Alchemy*'s Prolegomena (added here by al-Ghazzali, it does not appear in the *Revival)* where al-Ghazzali explores how to come to know the "self" in great detail.

*****

The traditional method of teaching a text is for the teacher to read it part by part with a class of students and then comment on what the text is saying. This is the method used next taking just the first subsection of Topic One of the Prolegomena, "Knowing Yourself" which appears in the following paragraphs in bold. The commentary and explanations that follow are enhanced with other sections of al-Ghazzali's writings in the *Alchemy* which are inset for clarity. If we were sitting in al-Ghazzali's classroom, this is the method he would be using.

NOTES TO THE INTRODUCTION

1 See works like *Timeless Healing: The Power and Biology of Belief* by Herbert Benson; *Why God Won't Go Away: Brain Science and the Biology of Belief* by Andrew Newberg, Eugene D'Aquili and Vince Rause; and *Handbook of Religion and Health* edited by Harold G. Koniz, Michael McCullough and David B. Larsen.

2 Other well known writers and poets born in Tus include Abu Yazid Bistami, Husayn bin Mansur Hallaj, Abu Said Abi'l-Khayr, Nizam al-Mulk, Firdawsi and Umar Khayyam.

3 See Bibliography to the Introduction for the numerous books that detail the life of al-Ghazzali. It is interesting to note that al-Ghazzali wrote the *Alchemy of Happiness* when the First Crusade ruled Jerusalem. Saladin arrived on the scene seventy-seven years after al-Ghazzali's death.

4 See below for the definition of traditional psychology which historically was called the science of ethics or practical wisdom (*hikmat al-amali*).

5 *Knowledge and the Sacred*, p. 68.

6 *Alchemy*, p. 841.

7 This is a clear distinction with modern secular psychology which is limited to only treating a human being part by part instead of holistically. See *Alchemy* p 817.

8 *Alchemy*, p 358.

9 *Alchemy*, p. 116.

10 *Alchemy*, p 525.

11 *Alchemy*, p 780.

12 *Alchemy*, p 358.

13 *Alchemy*, p 360.

14 *Alchemy*, pp 221-222.

15 *Ibid.*

BIBLIOGRAPHY

al-Ghazzali. *Ninety-nine Beautiful Names of God (al-Maqsad al-asna fi sharh asma Allah al-husna).* Translated by David B. Burrell and Nazih Daher. Cambridge: Islamic Texts Society, 1999.

Al-Ghazzali On Disciplining the Self. Translated from the *Alchemy of Happiness* by Muhammad Nur Abdus Salam (Jay R. Crook). Chicago: Kazi Publications, 2002.

al-Ghazzali. *On Disciplining the Soul and the Two Desires.* Translated from the *Ihya ulum al-din (Kitab riyadat al-nafs. Kitab kasr al-shahwatayn)* by T. J. Winter. Cambridge: Islamic Texts Society, 2001.

al-Ghazzali. *On Divine Predicates and their Properties (al-Iqtisad fil'itiqad).* Translated by Abdu Rahman Abu Zayd. India: Kitab Bhavan, 1994.

Al-Ghazzali On Earning a Living and Trade. Translated from *Alchemy of Happiness* by Muhammad Nur Abdus Salam (Jay R. Crook). Chicago: Kazi Publications, 2002.

Al-Ghazzali On Enjoining Good and Forbidding Wrong. Translated from *Alchemy of Happiness* by Muhammad Nur Abdus Salam (Jay R. Crook). Chicago: Kazi Publications, 2002.

Al-Ghazzali On Governing and Managing the State. Translated from *Alchemy of Happiness* by Muhammad Nur Abdus Salam (Jay R. Crook). Chicago: Kazi Publications, 2002.

Al-Ghazzali On Hope and Fear. Translated from *Alchemy of Happiness* by Muhammad Nur Abdus Salam (Jay R. Crook). Chicago: Kazi Publications, 2002.

Al-Ghazzali On Journeying. Translated from *Alchemy of Happiness* by Muhammad Nur Abdus Salam (Jay R. Crook). Chicago: Kazi Publications, 2002.

Al-Ghazzali On Knowing This World and the Hereafter. Translated from *Alchemy of Happiness* by Muhammad Nur Abdus Salam (Jay R. Crook). Chicago: Kazi Publications, 2002.

Al-Ghazzali On Knowing Yourself and God. Translated from *Alchemy of Happiness* by Muhammad Nur Abdus Salam (Jay R. Crook). Chicago: Kazi Publications, 2002.

Al-Ghazzali On Listening to Music. Translated from *Alchemy of Happiness* by Muhammad Nur Abdus Salam (Jay R. Crook). Chicago: Kazi Publications, 2002.

Al-Ghazzali On Love, Longing and Contentment. Translated from *Alchemy of Happiness* by Muhammad Nur Abdus Salam (Jay R. Crook). Chicago: Kazi Publications, 2002.

Al-Ghazzali On Marriage. Translated from *Alchemy of Happiness* by Muhammad Nur Abdus Salam (Jay R. Crook). Chicago: Kazi

26   *Alchemy of Happiness*

Publications, 2002.

Al-Ghazzali On Meditation. Translated from *Alchemy of Happiness* by
   Muhammad Nur Abdus Salam (Jay R. Crook). Chicago: Kazi
   Publications, 2002.

Al-Ghazzali On Patience and Gratitude. Translated from *Alchemy of
   Happiness* by Muhammad Nur Abdus Salam (Jay R. Crook). Chicago:
   Kazi Publications, 2002.

Al-Ghazzali On Reckoning and Guarding. Translated from *Alchemy of
   Happiness* by Muhammad Nur Abdus Salam (Jay R. Crook). Chicago:
   Kazi Publications, 2002.

Al-Ghazzali On Remembering Death and the States of the Hereafter.
   Translated from *Alchemy of Happiness* by Muhammad Nur Abdus Salam
   (Jay R. Crook). Chicago: Kazi Publications, 2002.

Al-Ghazzali On Repentance. Translated from *Alchemy of Happiness* by
   Muhammad Nur Abdus Salam (Jay R. Crook). Chicago: Kazi
   Publications, 2002.

Al-Ghazzali On Spiritual Poverty and Asceticism. Translated from *Alchemy of
   Happiness* by Muhammad Nur Abdus Salam (Jay R. Crook). Chicago:
   Kazi Publications, 2002.

Al-Ghazzali On Sufism. Translated from *Alchemy of Happiness* by
   Muhammad Nur Abdus Salam (Jay R. Crook). Chicago: Kazi
   Publications, 2002.

Al-Ghazzali On the Duties of Brotherhood. Translated from *Alchemy of
   Happiness* by Muhammad Nur Abdus Salam (Jay R. Crook). Chicago:
   Kazi Publications, 2002.

Al-Ghazzali On the Etiquette of Eating. Translated from *Alchemy of
   Happiness* by Muhammad Nur Abdus Salam (Jay R. Crook). Chicago:
   Kazi Publications, 2002.

al-Ghazzali. *On the Foundations of the Articles of Faith.* Translated from the
   Ihya ulum al-din (*Kitab qawaid al-aqaid*) by Nabih Amir Faris. Lahore:
   Sh. Muhammad Ashraf, 1999.

Al-Ghazzali On the Lawful, the Unlawful and the Doubtful. Translated from
   Alchemy of Happiness by Muhammad Nur Abdus Salam (Jay R. Crook).
   Chicago: Kazi Publications, 2002.

al-Ghazzali. *On the Manners Relating to Eating.* Translated from the *Ihya
   ulum al-din* (*Kitab adab al-akl*) by D. Johnson-Davies. Cambridge:
   Islamic Texts Society, 2000.

Al-Ghazzali On the Mysteries of the Pillars of Islam. Translated from *Alchemy
   of Happiness* by Muhammad Nur Abdus Salam (Jay R. Crook). Chicago:
   Kazi Publications, 2002.

Al-Ghazzali On the Treatment of Anger, Hatred and Envy. Translated from
   Alchemy of Happiness by Muhammad Nur Abdus Salam (Jay R. Crook).
   Chicago: Kazi Publications, 2002.

Al-Ghazzali On the Treatment of Hypocrisy. Translated from *Alchemy of Happiness* by Muhammad Nur Abdus Salam (Jay R. Crook). Chicago: Kazi Publications, 2002.

Al-Ghazzali On the Treatment of Ignorance Arising from Heedlessness, Error and Delusion. Translated from *Alchemy of Happiness* by Muhammad Nur Abdus Salam (Jay R. Crook). Chicago: Kazi Publications, 2002.

Al-Ghazzali On the Treatment of Love for This World. Translated from *Alchemy of Happiness* by Muhammad Nur Abdus Salam (Jay R. Crook). Chicago: Kazi Publications, 2002.

Al-Ghazzali On the Treatment of Love of Power and Control. Translated from *Alchemy of Happiness* by Muhammad Nur Abdus Salam (Jay R. Crook). Chicago: Kazi Publications, 2002.

Al-Ghazzali On the Treatment of Miserliness and Greed. Translated from *Alchemy of Happiness* by Muhammad Nur Abdus Salam (Jay R. Crook). Chicago: Kazi Publications, 2002.

Al-Ghazzali On the Treatment of Pride and Conceit. Translated from *Alchemy of Happiness* by Muhammad Nur Abdus Salam (Jay R. Crook). Chicago: Kazi Publications, 2002.

Al-Ghazzali On the Treatment of the Harms of the Tongue. Translated from *Alchemy of Happiness* by Muhammad Nur Abdus Salam (Jay R. Crook). Chicago: Kazi Publications, 2002.

Al-Ghazzali On the Treatment of the Lust of the Stomach and the Sexual Organs. Translated from *Alchemy of Happiness* by Muhammad Nur Abdus Salam (Jay R. Crook). Chicago: Kazi Publications, 2002.

Al-Ghazzali On Trust and the Unity of God. Translated from *Alchemy of Happiness* by Muhammad Nur Abdus Salam (Jay R. Crook). Chicago: Kazi Publications, 2002.

Al-Ghazzali On Truthfulness and Sincerity. Translated from *Alchemy of Happiness* by Muhammad Nur Abdus Salam (Jay R. Crook). Chicago: Kazi Publications, 2002.

al-Ghazzali. *Path to Sufism.* Translated by R. J. McCarthy. KY: fons vitae, 2001.

al-Ghazzali. *Some Moral and Religious Teachings.* Translated by Syed Nawab Ali. Lahore: Sh. Muhammad Ashraf, 1995.

al-Ghazzali. *Remembrance of Death and the Afterlife.* Translated from the *Ihya ulum al-din (Kitab dhikr al-mawt wa-ma-badahun)* by T. J. Winter. Cambridge: Islamic Texts Society, 1999.

al-Ghazzali. *The Duties of Brotherhood.* Translated from the *Ihya ulum al-din.* Leicester: Islamic Foundation, 1990.

al-Ghazzali. *The Mystic.* Margaret Smith. Chicago: Kazi Publications, 2002.

Avicenna. *The Canon of Medicine.* Chicago: Kazi Publications, 1999.

Benson, Herbert. *Timeless Healing: The Power and Biology of Belief.* NY: Simon and Schuster, 1996.

28   *Alchemy of Happiness*

Ethical Philosophy of al-Ghazzali. Muhammad Umar ud-Din. Lahore: Sh. Muhammad Ashraf, 1991.

Faith and Practice of al-Ghazzali. W. Montgomery Watt. Edinburgh: Edinburgh University Press, 1952. An abridged translation of *Munqidh min ad-dalal* (Deliverance from Error) and the Beginning of Guidance (*Bidayat al-hidayah*).

Fakhry, Majid. *Al-Ghazzali's Theory of Virtue.* NY: SUNY, 1985.

Koniz, Harold G., Michael McCullough and David B. Larsen. *Handbook of Religion and Health.* NY: Oxford University Press, 2001.

Newberg, Andrew, Eugene D'Aquili and Vince Rause. *Why God Won't Go Away: Brain Science and the Biology of Belief.* NY: Ballantine Books, 2002.

AL-GHAZZALI ON HOPE AND FEAR

Know that hope (*raja*) and fear (*khawf*) are like two wings for the traveler of the way; whatever praiseworthy stations he reaches, he does so by their strength, for the obstacles which veil the Divine Presence are extremely high. So long as hope is not truthful and the eye does not fall upon the beauty of the Divine Presence, one cannot overcome those obstacles. The appetites on the road of hell are usually deceptive and crushing; their nets are attractive and difficult. So long as alarm does not overcome the heart, one cannot avoid them. It is for this reason that the grace of fear and hope is great. Hope is as the bridle that draws on the servant of God, while fear is as the whip by which he is driven. Let us first discuss the effect of hope, and then the effect of fear.

1 THE TRUE NATURE OF HOPE

Know that the worship of God Most High in the hope of grace and generosity is better than worship in anxiety about punishment; for love rises from hope, and no station is higher than love, while the dread of abhorrence is from fear. It is for this that the Messenger (ﷺ) said: "Let not one of you die while he does not have a good opinion of God Most High." And he said that God Most High says: "I am there where (My) servant thinks. Say: Think whatever thought you wish about Me."

And the Messenger (☾) said to someone at the time of death: "How do you find yourself?" (The dying man) said: "It is as though I fear because of my sins and I hope for His mercy." (The Messenger) (☾) said: "There is no one at such a moment in whose heart both are not joined that God Most High does not grant him security from that which he fears and grants (him) that for which he hopes."

God Most High sent a revelation to Jacob (☾): "Do you know why I separated Joseph (☾) from you for so many years? Because you said: '*I fear lest the wolf devour him.*' (Q. 12:13) Why did you fear the wolf and not have hope in Me? You thought about the carelessness of his brothers, but you did not think about My guardianship." And Ali, may God be pleased with him, saw someone hopeless because of his many sins. (Ali) said: "Despair not, for His mercy is greater than your sins."

The Messenger (☾) said: "On the Day of Resurrection God Most High shall say to (His) servant: 'Why did you not take action against the evil that you saw?' If God Most High calls his tongue to witness, it will say: 'I feared the people and had hope of Thy mercy.' God Most High will have mercy upon him." And one day the Messenger (☾) said: "If you knew what I know, you would weep much and laugh little. You would go to the desert and you would beat your breasts and you would wail." Then Gabriel came and said: "God Most High says: 'Why dost thou make My people despair of My mercy?'" So he came out and by God's grace gave (the people) good hopes (for God's mercy).

God Most High send a revelation to David (☾): "Make Me beloved in the hearts of (My) servants." (David) asked: "How can I make them into friends?" (God) answered: "Remind them of My favors and blessings, for they have experienced nothing from Me save My goodness."

Yahya bin Aktham was seen in a dream. He was asked:

"What has God Most High done with you and how?" He answered: "He kept me in the station of interrogation and said: 'O shaykh, you did such and such,' until I was overwhelmed by a great dread. Then I said: 'O Lord God, I was not given such information about Thee.' He said: 'How was the information you were given?' I said: "Abd al-Razzaq gave me such information (having heard it) from Zuhri, (who heard it) from Anis, (who heard it) from Thy Messenger Muhammad (ﷺ), (who heard it) from Gabriel, (who heard it) from Thee Who said: "I shall do with My servant what he thinks of Me and expects from Me." And I had the expectation that Thou wouldst have mercy upon me.' God Most High and Sanctified said: 'Zuhri spoke the truth and My Messenger spoke the truth and Gabriel spoke the truth. I have had mercy upon you.' Then I was dressed in a wondrous robe and after that the servants of Paradise went before me. I experienced a happiness of which there is no likeness."

In the Traditions it is related that one of the Children of Israel used to cause the people to despair of the mercy of God Most High and would make things very hard for them. On the Day of Resurrection, God Most High will say to him: "This day I shall make thee as despairing of My mercy as thou didst make My people despair of it."

And in the Traditions it is related that a man is in hell for a thousand years and then he says: "O Compassionate! O Benefactor!" God Most High says to Gabriel: Go and bring My servant." When he has been brought, (God) asks him: "How didst thou find thy place in hell?" He answers: "The worst of places." (God) says: "Carry him back to hell." As they are carrying him off, he looks back. From God Most High comes a call: "Why dost thou look back?" He answers: "O Lord God, I thought that after Thou hadst brought me out of hell, Thou wouldst not send me back to hell." (God) declares: "Take him to Paradise!" He obtains salvation with that thought and hope.

Know that whoever is optimistic about the future, that optimism which he has is called hope. It may also be called desire; or it may be called delusion or stupidity. The fools do not distinguish one of these from another and suppose that all of these are hope, and that this hope is praiseworthy, while that is not the case. Indeed, if a person seeks good seed and sows it in soft earth and cleans it of thorns and weeds and gives it water at the proper times and hopes that he will reap a harvest and that God Most High will withhold the lightning; this optimism is called hope. But if one sows rotten seed on the hard ground and does not clean out the thorns and weeds and does not give it water, but hopes that rain will fall in a place where it usually does not rain—but it also not impossible—this is called wish and desire. In the same way, whoever plants the seed of correct faith on the plain of the breast and cleans the breast of the thorns of bad traits and irrigates the tree of faith with care in devotion and hopes that the grace of God Most High will repel disasters and that it will stay that way until the time of death and bear his faith soundly (to the Hereafter); this is called hope.

Its sign is that in the future one commits no fault nor withholds (one's) caretaking, as far as possible; for laying down the caretaking of tillage is from despair, not from hope. However if the seed of faith is corrupted so that (its) certainty is not sound, or it is sound but the breast has not been cleansed of bad traits and devotion has not been watered, expecting the mercy of God Most High is stupidity, not hope. As the Messenger (ﷺ) said: "The fool is one who himself follows the impulses of his animal soul and who desires of God, may He be honored and glorified, his longings." The fool is he who does whatever he wants and expects (God's) mercy. Indeed, God Most High said: And a generation has succeeded them who inherited the Scriptures. They grasp the goods of this low life and say: '*It will be forgiven us*.' (Q. 7:169) He reproached those persons who, after the prophets had delivered knowledge to them but they had become immersed in the world, said: "We expect that God Most High will have mercy upon us."

Therefore, when anything has been exhausted, the necessaries of which are related to the discretion of a servant (of God), the fruit of expectation is hope. When the necessaries are destroyed, the fruit of expectation is stupidity and delusion. If they are not destroyed, but not in good form, (the fruit of expectation) is wishing. The Messenger (ﷺ) said: "There is no religion in desiring." The task of religion is not managed with wishing. So, whoever repents must hold the hope of acceptance. For whoever does not repent, but is sorrowful and troubled because of his sinning and has the expectation that God Most High will accept his repentance, there is the hope that his misery will be the cause that will draw him to repentance. However, if he is not sorrowful and hopes for repentance, it is delusion. If he hope for forgiveness without repentance, it is in the same way delusion, even if fools call this hope. God Most High says: *Lo! Those who believe, and those who emigrate and strive in the Way of God, these have hope of God's mercy.* (Q. 2:218) Those have accepted the faith and who have left their wishes in their own cities and habitations and have chosen expatriation and who have striven against the unbelievers-for them there is cause to hope of My mercy.

Yahya Muadh says: "There is no stupidity greater than that of the one who strews live coals and expects Paradise and seeks the mansion of the devout while he performs the works of the rebels (against God), or hopes for spiritual reward for unperformed works."

There was a person called Zayd al-Khayl. He said to the Messenger (ﷺ): "I have come to you to ask what the sign that

God Most High wishes well for a person is, and what the sign that He does not wish well for him is." (The Messenger) answered: "Every day when you arise, how are you?" (Zayd) said: "As though I love goodness and the doers of good. If some good appears, I perform it quickly and I recognize its spiritual reward with certainty. It if passes me by, I become miserable and remain unhappy in the desire for that." (The Messenger) said: "This is the sign that He has wished well for you. If He had wanted the other, He would have engaged you in it and then there would not have been any dread as to in which of the valleys of the world He would have destroyed you."

(1) THE REMEDY FOR OBTAINING HOPE

Know that no one has need of this medicine except for two ailing persons: one is he who has become despairing because of the multitude of his sins and he does not repent, saying that it would not be accepted. The other is he who destroys himself with the multitude of his efforts and devotions and the many pains he imposes upon himself which he cannot endure. These two sick persons are in need of this medicine. However, this medicine is not for the heedless. Hope overcomes for two reasons:

(1) The first reason is taking a lesson. One reflects upon the wonders of the world and upon the creation of plants, animals, and the different kinds of blessings—as we have discussed previously in the Book on Gratitude—until one perceives a mercy, favor, and kindness which cannot be exceeded. Indeed, if one examines oneself and how He has created everything one would need, even that which is absolutely necessary such as the head and heart; or that which is not absolutely necessary such as hands and feet; or how He has created that which is adornment such as the redness of the lips, the arch of

the eyebrows, or the blackness and straightness of the eyelashes. He has performed this mercy upon all animals: even on the bee there are many delicacies of (His) handiwork in the symmetry of its form and the beauty of its coloring, and the guidance which He has given it so that it builds its own house and in which it stores honey, and in how it obeys its queen, and how their queen makes policy. Whoever meditates upon such marvels, external and internal, in himself and in all created things, knows that mercy is greater than that which would allow room for despair or that fear should overcome (one).

Instead, fear and hope should be equal; so if hope overcomes, there is room for that. The signs of the kindness and mercy of God Most High in creation themselves have no limit so that one of the saints says that there is no verse in the Quran offering more hope than the Verse of Lending and Borrowing (Q. 2:282), for God Most High revealed the longest verse in the Quran in order to preserve our property so that it would not be lost by giving loans. This is one remedy for obtaining hope and it is of very infinite greatness, but not everyone can attain that degree.

(2) The second reason is meditation upon the verses and Traditions of hope, which are also beyond numbering. As in the Quran it is said that no one should despair of "My mercy": *Despair not of the mercy of God.* (Q. 39:53) The angels will ask for your forgiveness: *(The angels) ask forgiveness for those on earth.* (Q. 42:5) Hell is for the purpose of keeping the unbelievers in it; but you are tormented and frightened by it: *With this God does appall His servants.* (Q. 39:16) And the Messenger (ﷺ) was not content with begging forgiveness of his people day and night until this verse was revealed: *Truly thy Lord is rich in pardon for mankind despite their wrongdoing.* (Q. 13:6) When the verse was revealed: *And verily the Lord will give unto thee so that thou will be content,* (Q. 93:5)

He said that Muhammad would not be satisfied so long as one of his people was in hell. There are many such verses.

As for the Traditions, the Messenger says: "My people are immune (*mahrum*); their punishment will be in the world: turmoil and earthquakes. When the Day of Resurrection comes an unbeliever will be handed over to each one and (the Muslim) will be told: 'This one is your sacrifice in hell.'" And he said: "Fever is a heat-prostration from hell; that is the portion of the believer from hell."

Anas says: "The Messenger (ﷺ) said: 'O Lord God, make the accounting of my people with me lest anyone see their bad deeds.' (God) said: 'They are thy peoples and My servants. I am more merciful with them. I do not desire that anyone see their bad deeds; neither thou, nor another.'"

And the Messenger (ﷺ) said: "My life is good for you and my death is good for you. If I am alive, I teach you the Religious Law; if I am dead, your deeds will be displayed before me. I shall praise and give thanks for those which are good and I shall ask forgiveness for those which are bad."

One day the Messenger (ﷺ) said: "O Generous in Pardoning!" Gabriel (ﷺ) said: "Do you know what the meaning of that is? It is that He pardon the unseemly and exchange it for goodness."

He (ﷺ) said: "When a servant of God sins and asks forgiveness, God Most High says: 'O angels, look! My servant has sinned and he knows that he has a Master Who will not take him for the sin but will forgive him. I take you to bear witness that I have forgiven him.'"

And he (ﷺ) said: "God Most High says: 'If one of My servants sins to the extend of the heavens and the earth, I shall forgive him when he asks for forgiveness and puts his hope in Me.' And He said: 'If a servant has sins to the fill the earth, I have mercy for him to fill the earth.'"

And he (ﷺ) said: "An angel does not record the sin against

a servant of God until six hours have passed. If he repents and asks forgiveness, (the angel) records nothing. If he does not repent but he asks forgiveness and performs devotions, the angel on his right hand says to the other (angel): 'Discard this sin from his record as I shall discard too a good deed in exchange for that. Every good deed (counts) for ten. Nine will remain for him.'"

And he (ﷺ) said: "When a servant of God commits a sin it is recorded against him." A desert Arab asked: "If he repents?" (The Messenger) answered: "It is erased." (The desert Arab) asked: "If he returns to that?" (The Messenger) said: "It is recorded." (The Arab) asked: "And if he repents?" (The Messenger) said: "It is erased." (The Arab) asked: "For how long?" (The Messenger) replied: "As long as he seeks forgiveness. God Most High does not tire of forgiving so long as (His) servant does not tire of asking forgiveness. When one intends to do a good deed, the angel records a good deed before it is performed. If he performs it, (the angel) records 'ten'; then he increases it up to seven hundred. When one intends to commit a sin, (the angel) does not record anything; if one commits it, (the angel) records 'one'; and there is the hope of the pardon of God Most High."

A man said to the Messenger (ﷺ): "I fast the month of Ramadan and perform the daily five obligatory formal prayers, but I do not exceed that. I am not obligated to pay the poor rate or to go on pilgrimage because I have no property. Shall I be with you on the Day of Resurrection?" The Messenger (ﷺ) smiled and said: "You will be with me if you preserve your heart from two things: from fostering enmity and envy; if you restrain your tongue from two things: slander and lies; and if you must restrain your eyes from two things: looking at those of the prohibited degrees and looking at the servants of God Most High with contempt. You will enter

Paradise together with me and I shall hold you dearer than this, the palm of my own hand."

A desert Arab asked the Messenger (ﷺ): "O Messenger of God, who will take the account of the people in the Hereafter?"[83] (the Messenger) answered: "God Most High." (The man) said: "He Himself?" (The Messenger) said: "Yes, He Himself." The desert Arab laughed. The Messenger (ﷺ) said: "Do you laugh, O man of the desert!" (The other) replied: "Yes, for when the Generous obtains, He pardons; when He reckons, He is lenient." The Messenger said: "You speak correctly, for there is no one more generous than God Most High." Then he added: "This desert Arab is a jurisprudent!" Then the Messenger said: "God Most High has made the Kabah noble and great. If someone were to destroy the Kabah and pull it down stone by stone and burn it, his crime would not be of the degree of that were he to make light of one of the friends of God Most High." The desert Arab asked: "Who are the friends of God?" He answered: "All believers are His friends. Have you not heard the verse: *God is the Friend of those who believe; He brings them out from darkness into light?*" (Q. 2:257)

And he said: "God Most High says: 'I created mankind so that they would benefit from Me, not so that I would benefit from them.'" And he said: "Before He created mankind, God Most High prescribed upon Himself: 'My mercy precedes My anger.'" And he said: "Whoever has said "there is no god but God" in sincerity shall go heaven. Whoever whose last words are those shall not see hellfire. Whoever goes to the next world without ascribing partnership to God shall not enter the fire." And he (ﷺ) said: "If you had not sinned, God Most High would have created another people so that they might sin in order (for Him) to forgive them; for He is Forgiving and Compassionate." And he said: "God Most High is more merciful to His servant than a mother is kind to her child."

And he (ﷺ) said: "God Most High will show as much

mercy on the Day of Resurrection such as the heart of any of
His servants has never experienced, to such an extent that
Iblis will raise his head in the hope of mercy." And he (ﷺ) said:
"God Most High has one hundred mercies: He has put aside
ninety-nine until the Day of Resurrection and not revealed
more than one mercy in this world. All hearts are merciful by
that one mercy, even the mercy of the mother for her child and
the mercy of the animal for its young; all are from that one
mercy! On the Day of Resurrection, that one mercy will join
the ninety-nine and be spread over mankind, each mercy as
great as the storeys of the heavens and the earth. No one will
be destroyed on that Day except those who are destroyed in
eternity without beginning." And he (ﷺ) said: "I have reserved
my intercession for the committers of major sins among my
people; do not suppose that it is for the devout and the pious;
rather, it is for the polluted and the confused."

Sad bin Bilal said: "Two men are brought out of hell on the
Day of Resurrection. God Most High says: 'That which you
have suffered you suffered for your evil deeds, for I do not
oppress My Own servants.' And He commands that they be
taken back to hell. One of the two goes off hurriedly in chains
and irons while the other hangs back. (God) commands that
both be brought back. He asks him who had hurried: 'Why
didst thou do thus?' (The man) replies: "I was afraid. Because
of the punishment I have experienced for (my) disobedience, I
did not have the audacity to pause when the command came."
And the other says: "I had a happy thought and I hoped that
since Thou hadst brought me out of hell, Thou wouldst not
send me back.' For these reasons, He sent both of them to
Paradise."

And the Messenger (ﷺ) said: "On the Day of Resurrection
a Crier will cry out: 'O people of Muhammad, I have done what
is Mine with regard to your affair, but your claims over one
another remain (to be settled). Do this to one another and

enter Paradise.'" And he (ﷺ) said: "On the Day of Resurrection, one of my people will be brought up before all mankind and ninety-nine ledgers. As far as the eye can see, he will see only sins. God, may He honored and glorified, asks: 'Dost thou deny any of all these (sins) and have the angels been unjust in recording them?' He answers: 'No, O Lord.' (God) asks: 'Hast thou any excuse?' He answers: 'No, O Lord,' and he sets his heart on hell. God says: 'I have a good deed of thine and I oppress thee not.' Then a piece of paper is brought forward upon which is written: I testify that there is not god but God and I testify that Muhammad is the Messenger of God. Then the servant of God asks: 'How can this piece of paper suffice for all those ledgers?' (God) says: 'They are not unfair to thee. They place all of those ledgers in one pan of the scales and that piece of paper in the other pan. And that piece of paper, which is heavier than all (in the other pan), causes all (of thy sins) to be lifted away; for nothing overcomes the Unity of God Most High.'"

And he (ﷺ) said: "On the Day of Resurrection, God Most High commands the angels to bring out of hell anyone in whose heart there is mustard seed's (weight) of goodness. They bring many out. Then they say: "No one of this class of people remains." (God) says: 'Bring out anyone in whose heart there is half a mustard seed's (weight) of goodness.' They bring out many more. The Fire says: 'None of these people are left.' Then He says: 'Bring out everyone in whose heart there is an atom of goodness.' Throngs of people are brought out and they say that no one with an atom of goodness in him remains. The intercession of the angels and prophets and the believers has all been completed and has been answered. Nothing is left for the mercy of the Most Merciful of the Merciful. He takes a handful out of hell and brings out some believers who had never done any good, even an atom's worth; all had become as black as charcoal. He throws them into one of the streams of

heaven, that which is called the River of Life. They come out
of that pure and bright, as greens that come from the midst of
flowing waters, shining like pearls with small stones about
the neck so that the inhabitants of heaven may recognize
them. They say: 'These are all those liberated by God Most
High who have done no good deeds.' Then He will say: 'Enter
Paradise; all that ye see is yours.' They will say: 'O Lord God,
Thou hast given us what Thou hast not given any of the inhabitants of heaven.' He will say: 'Ye are greater to Me than that.'
They will say: 'O Lord God, what is greater than this?' He will
say: 'My satisfaction, for I am pleased with you, for I never
become displeased.'" This Tradition is found in the *Sahih* of
Bukhari and the *Sahih* of Muslim.

Amr bin Hazm says that the Messenger was absent for
three days, coming out (of his house) for nothing except the
obligatory formal prayers. When it was the fourth day, he
came out and said: "God Most High given me promise, saying:
'I shall forgive 70,000 of your people without reckoning and
place them in heaven.' During these three days I begged for
more. I found God Most High magnanimous and generous; for
each one of those 70,000, He gave me 70,000 more. I said: 'O
God! How many shall my people be?' He said: 'I shall complete
this number from all of the wandering Arabs (*arab*).'"

It is related that a child was captured in one of the expe-
ditions in defense of the faith and was placed for auction on a
very hot day. The eye of a woman in a tent fell upon that child
and she ran out and the people in that tent ran out after her.
She snatched the child up and clasped it to her breast and
gave it shade with her own body so that heat would not affect
it. She cried: "This is my son." When the people saw this they
wept and left off their work because of her great compassion.
Then the Messenger (ﷺ) arrived there and was told the story
of what had happened. He rejoiced at their compassion and
their weeping, and he said: "Are you astonished by the com-

passion and mercy of this woman for the boy?" They said: 'Yes, O Messenger of God." He said: "God Most High is more merciful upon all than this woman is for her own son." Then the Muslims dispersed from that place with a joy the like of which there had never been.

Ibrahim Adham, may God have mercy upon him, said: "One night I was circumambulating (the Kabah) by myself and it was raining. I said: 'O Lord God, preserve me from sin so that I have no fault.' I heard a voice from the direction of the Kabah. It said: 'Thou desirest sinlessness *(ismat)* and all My servants desire that very sinlessness. If I keep all from sinning, then to whom shall I make known My grace and mercy?'"

Know that there are many such Traditions, and let them be the cure of the person whose fear overwhelms him. The person who is dominated by heedlessness must understand that in all of these Traditions it is apparent that some believers will go to hell. The hindmost person will be the one who comes out of hell after seven thousand years. Since it is possible with respect to any person that he be that one, one must take up the way of resoluteness and circumspection. As much as one can, one must strive not to be that person. If one passes up all the pleasures of the world in that fear so that one not have to be one night in hell, it would be fit; so what could one say about seven thousand years?

In short, fear and hope should be in balance, as Umar, may God be pleased with him, said: "If it is announced that tomorrow no one will enter Paradise save one person, I shall think that I may be that one person; and if it is said that no one will enter hell save one person, I shall think that I will be that person. "

2 THE TRUE NATURE OF FEAR OF GOD

Know that fear if one of the great stations and its virtue is appropriate to its causes and its results.

As for its causes, they are knowledge and gnosis (*marifat*), as will be explained after this. About this, God Most High said: *Those of His servants only who are possessed of knowledge fear God.* (Q. 35:28) And the Messenger (ﷺ) said: "The heighth of wisdom is the fear of God.

As for its results, they are temperance, Godliness, and piety. All of these are seeds of (spiritual) happiness, for one cannot travel the way to the Hereafter without surrendering lust and (without possessing) patience. Nothing burns away appetite like fear. It is for this that God Most High has combined for the Godfearing guidance, mercy, knowledge, and pleasure and sent three verses in the Quran. The first is: *A guidance and mercy for those who fear their Lord.* (Q. 7:154) Another is: *Those of His servants only who are possessed of knowledge fear God.* (Q. 35:28) And He said: *God is pleased with them and they are pleased with Him; this is for him who fears God.* (Q. 98:8) Piety, which God Most High has joined to Himself, is a result of fear. He said: . . . *but piety from you reaches Him.* (Q. 22:37)

And the Messenger (ﷺ) said: "That day on which mankind will be gathered on the plain of the Resurrection, a Crier shall address them in a voice heard far and near, saying: 'O people, I have heard all your words from the day on which I created (you), so today listen to My words and pay attention, for I shall place your affair before you. O people, ye have set down a lineage (*nasab*) and I have set down a lineage. Ye have exalted your lineage and have dismissed My lineage. I have said: Lo! *The noblest of you in the sight of God is the most Godfearing;* (Q. 49:13)—the greatest among you is the most pious. Ye say: 'Great is that person who is so-and-so the son of so-and-so.' Today I exalt My lineage and dismiss your lineage. Where are the Godfearing? Where are the devout?' Then a banner will be raised and brought forward, and the devout will follow after it until all have entered Paradise without accounting." It is for this reason that He doubled the spiritual reward of the fearing when He said: *But for him who fears the standing before his Lord there are two gardens.* (Q. 55:46)

The Messenger (ﷺ) said: "God Most High says: 'By My power, I do not impose two fears and two securities upon a single servant. If he fears me in the world, I shall make him secure in the Hereafter; but if he is secure (in the world), I shall keep him in fear in the Hereafter.'" And the Messenger (ﷺ) said: "Whoever fears God Most High, all things fear him; whoever does not fear God Most High is frightened by everything." And he said: "The one with the most perfect intelligence among you is the one who fears God Most High the most." And he said: "There is no believer who sheds a single tear drop because of fearing God Most High—even if it is in the amount of a fly's wing that touches his cheek—whose face is not forbidden to the Fire." And he said: "When the hair of a servant of God stands up because of his fearing God Most High, and he thinks upon that, his sins fall away as leaves from a tree." And he said: "Everyone who weeps because of fear of God Most High will not go into the Fire, so long as milk which comes out the breast will not flow back (into the breast)."

Ayishah, may God be pleased with her, says: "I asked the Messenger (ﷺ) whether any of his people would enter heaven without accounting. He answered: 'Yes, he who trembles when remembering his sins.'" And said the Messenger (ﷺ): "No drop is more beloved by God Most High than the tear drop that is shed out of the fear of God and the drop of blood which is shed in the way of God Most High." And he said: "There will be seven persons in the shade of the Throne of God Most High on the Day of Resurrection: one among these seven is the person who weeps when remembering God Most High in private." Hanzalah says: "I was with the Messenger (ﷺ) and he was counseling us so that hearts had become attenuated and tears were flowing. Then I returned home and my family began to talk and I became immersed in worldly talk. Then I recalled the words of the Messenger (ﷺ) and I came out because of my weeping and I was shouting: 'Ah! Hanzalah has become a hypocrite.' Abu Bakr, may God be pleased with him, appeared and said: 'You have not become a hypocrite.' I went to the Messenger (ﷺ) and said: 'Hanzalah has become a hypocrite.' He said: 'Of course Hanzalah has not become a hypocrite!' Then I recounted my story. He said: 'O Hanzalah, if you continued as you were when you were with me, angels would take your hand on the roads and in houses; but, O Hanzalah, hour by hour.'"

Non-prophetic traditions: Shibli, may God have mercy upon him, says: "There never was a day in which fear (of God) overwhelmed me that one of the gates of wisdom was not opened to me." Yahya bin Muadh says: "The sin of a believer is between the fear of punishment and the hope of mercy like a fox between two lions." He also said: "If the destitute person would fear hell as he fears poverty, he would enter heaven." He was asked: "Who will be more fortunate tomorrow?" He answered: "He who is more frightened today." Someone asked Hasan Basri: "What do you say about the public assembly that frightens us so much that our hearts are torn apart?" He said: "It is better that you tell the people: 'You are frightened today so that you will attain security tomorrow,' than that you tell the people: 'You have security today and you will attain fear tomorrow.'" Abu Sulayman Darani says: "No heart is free from fear that is not in ruins."

Ayishah said: "I asked the Messenger (ﷺ): 'What is that which is said in the Quran they do and they fear: *They give what they give with hearts afraid* (Q. 23:60). Is this theft or adultery?' He said: 'No, they perform obligatory formal prayer, they keep the fast, and they give in charity and they fear that it will not be accepted (by God).'" Muhammad bin Munkadir, when weeping, would rub his tears (on his face) and would say: "I have heard that every place the tears reach will never burn." (Abu Bakr) the Truly Righteous says: "Weep and if you cannot, make yourself." Kab Ahbar says: "By God, let me weep so that the water flows on my face. I prefer that to giving a few heaps of gold to the poor." Abd Allah bin Umar says: "I prefer one tear drop shed out of fear of God Most High over giving a thousand dinars in charity."

Know that fear too is one of the states of the heart and it is the fire of a pain that appears in the heart. It has causes and results.

As for its causes, they are knowledge and gnosis,. because one understands the danger of the affair of the Hereafter and one understands that the causes of one's destruction are pre-pared and overpowering. This fire of pain necessarily appears in the midst of his spirit (*jan*) and arises from two types of gnosis (*marifat*):

(1) One is that one truly sees his own defects, his own sins, the blights upon his acts of devotion, the malignancies of his character; and with these faults, he sees the blessings of God Most High upon himself. He is like the person who has received robes of honor and favors from a king, and then has betrayed (the king) in his family quarters and treasury. Then he suddenly realizes that the king has seen him in his treach-eries and he knows that the king is jealous, avenging, and fearless. (The man) knows no one close to the king to intercede on his behalf. He has neither means nor relationship. The fire of pain will necessarily appear in his heart when he sees the imperilment of his own affair.

(2) As for the second type of gnosis or insight, it does not spring from his attributes; rather, it springs from fearlessness and its power, which he fears. Just as when a person falls into the claws of a lion and is afraid, not because of his own sin, but

because he knows about the nature of the lion which is about
to kill and that it has no fear him and his weakness. This fear
is more total and superior. And whoever knows the attributes
of God Most High and has come to recognize His Majesty,
Greatness, and Fearlessness—for if He destroys the entire
world and keeps it in hell eternally, not one atom of His kingdom would be diminished—and His essence is above the reality of that which is called kindness and compassion; there is
room for him to be afraid. The prophets had this fear too, even
though they knew they were innocent of sins. Whoever
becomes more familiar with God Most High because more
frightened. The Messenger (ﷺ) said about this: "I am the most
knowing of God among you and the most fearing." For this
reason He said: *Those of His servants only who are possessed
of knowledge fear God.* (Q. 35:28) The more ignorant a person
is, the more secure he feels. A revelation came to David (ﷺ):
"O David, fear Me as you would fear an enraged lion." This is
the cause of fear.

As for the results of fear, they are (1) in the heart, (2) in
the body, and (3) in the limbs.

(1) As for those in the heart, they make lust or the carnal
appetites loathsome to one and there is no care for them. For
if a person has a craving for a woman or some food, when he
falls into the claws of a lion or into the prison of a harsh ruler,
no care about that appetite is left to him. Rather, the state of
his heart in fear is total humility, submissiveness, and abject-
ness; it is all observation, calculation, and looking at conse-
quences. No pride remains, neither envy, appetite for the
world, nor heedlessness.

(2) As for its results in the body, they are emaciation and
pallor.

(3) And its results in the (bodily) limbs are keeping them
pure from sins and making them obedient in devotion (to
God).

The degrees of fear are various: if it keeps one from the lust, it is called temperance; if it keeps one from the unlawful, it is called self-restraint; if it keeps one from the doubtful or from the lawful from fear of the unlawful, it is called piety ; if it keeps one from everything except the provisions for the road to the Hereafter; it is called truth and the person is called truly righteous. Temperance and self-restraint are beneath piety and all of these are beneath truth. In reality, this is fear. As for him who weeps and shaves (his head) and says: "There is no power nor strength except with God," and then goes back to his heedlessness, this is called the weakheartedness of women. This is not fear, for whoever fears something flees from it. A person who has something in his sleeve looks to see whether it is a snake; it is not possible for him to content himself with "there is no power (nor strength except with God)"; rather, he throws it down. Dhul-Nun was asked: "Who is the fearing servant of God?" He replied: "He who feigns sickness so that he may avoid all carnal appetites because of the fear of death."

(1) THE DEGREES OF FEAR

Know that for fear, too, there are three degrees: weak, strong, and moderate. The most praiseworthy of them is moderate. Weak is that which does not prompt a person to act, such as the mildness of women. Strong is that from which there is the fear of hopelessness, the fear of illness, losing consciousness, and death. Both of these are blameworthy, for fear in itself is not a perfection as (are) the Divine Unity, gnosis, and love. It is for this that it is not included among the attributes of God Most High. Moreover, there is no fear without ignorance and feebleness, for so long as the outcome is unknown and there is no inability to avoid peril, there is no fear. But, fear is perfect when it is joined to the state of the heedless. It is like the whip which instructs children and moves animals on their way. When it is so weak that there is not sufficient pain, it is not instructive nor does it direct on the way; or when it is too strong children and animals are injured or (bones are) broken. Neither of these are beneficial; rather, it should be (applied) in moderation so as to restrain one from sin and make one eager for devotion.

The fear of whoever is more learned is more moderate, for when it becomes excessive he reflects again upon the causes of hope; when it becomes weak he reflects again upon the dangers of the affair. Whoever does not fear and calls himself learned, has learned that which is useless, not knowledge; like the fortune-teller in the market who calls himself a wise man, but has no hint of wisdom. The beginning of all gnoses (*marifat-ha*) is that one come to know oneself and God Most High: oneself with (one's) defects and shortcomings, and God Most High with His Greatness, Majesty, and His not being afraid to destroy the world. Nothing is born from these two insights other than fear. It is for this that the Messenger (ﷺ) said: "The beginning of knowledge is the insight into the Omnipotent and the end of knowledge is entrusting the affair to Him." He said: The beginning of knowledge is that you know the God by His omnipotence and vanquishing; and the end is that, servant-like, you entrust your affair to Him and that you know that you are nothing and that you have nothing. How would it be possible that a person know this and not fear?

(II) THE KINDS OF FEAR

Know that fear arises from the knowledge of danger; each person has a different danger before him. There is the person to whom hell comes before him, and his fear is of that. There is the person to whom something comes which is on the path to hell, so that he fears that he may die before he repents; or he fears that he may fall into sin again; or that hardness and heedlessness may appear in his heart; or that his habits may carry him to the threshold of sin; or his vanity may overcome him because of his blessings; or that he may be caught on the Day of Resurrection because of his oppressions of the people; or that his scandals may become public and he be disgraced; or he fears that something may occur in his thought that God Most High sees and knows and of which He does not approve.

The benefit of each of these is that one work upon that which he fears. When he fears (bad) habits will carry him to sin, he flees from the path of (those) habits. When he fears the knowledge of God Most High, he keeps his heart pure. In the same way, the most overwhelming to his fearful heart is the fear of the conclusion, lest he not take his faith (with him) intact (to the Hereafter). More perfect than this is the fear of the past as to what has been decided with respect to his tribulations or happiness, for the conclusion is the corollary of the past. The reality is that which the Messenger (ﷺ) said from the pulpit: "God Most High has written a book and the names of the inhabitants of Paradise are in it." He raised his right hand and he said: "He has written another book, and the names of the inhabitants of hell together with their lineage and particulars are in it." He raised his left hand and he said: "There will be no increase nor any reduction in them. And there are of the people of happiness those who perform the deeds of the wretched, so that all will say that he is of (one of the wretched condemned to hell). Then God Most High will turn him away from that road before his death-even if it is but an hour away-and bring him to the road to happiness. Happy is he who is happy in the eternal decree and wretched is he who is wretched in the eternal decree, but the (important) matter is the ending."

Therefore, for this reason, the fear of the wisdom is of this and that is more perfect, just as fear of God Most High by reason of the attributes of His Majesty is more perfect than the fear by reason of one's own sins; for that fear will never depart. When one fears sin, it may be lead to the delusion: "Since I have stopped sinning, what have I to fear?"

In short, whoever recognizes that the Messenger (ﷺ) will be at the highest of the degrees and Abu Jahl in the lowest degree of hell though neither possessed any means or crime prior to creation. When He created (them), He made easy the way of gnosis and devotion to the Messenger, causelessly on his part. It was made necessary that his desire be used for that; he would not have been able to conceal from himself that which was shown and revealed to him. He would have been unable to distance himself from that which he knew to be a fatal poison. But Abu Jahl, whose vision was shut off, was unable to perceive. Since he did not see, he was unable to hold himself back from appetites without recognizing their detriment. So both were compelled. However, as He intended, He commanded one to wretchedness causelessly and drove him to hell. He commanded one to happiness and carried him to the highest of the high with the chain of force. Whoever issues such commands as He wishes has no fear, but fearing Him is inevitable. It is for this that He said to David (ﷺ): "Fear Me as you would fear a roaring lion," for a lion does not fear to destroy. If it stops, it is not because of compassion or anxiety that it releases you, but because of your unimportance to it. It is not possible for whoever has understood these attributes of God Most High to be free from fear. And God is the Best Knower.

(III) THE BAD ENDING

Know that most of the fearful have been afraid of the ending, because the human heart is (constantly) changing and the time of death is an awesome moment. It is not possible to

know what it will settle upon at that time. One of the spiritu-
ally insightful of religion even says: "If I have known a person
(to be) in the Unity (of God) for fifty years, since he has been
absent from me many times behind walls, I cannot swear to
his (adherence to the creed of Divine) Unity, because the condition of the heart is changeable. I do not know into what it
may turn." Another says: "If they say: 'Do you prefer martyrdom at the door of (your) house or death as a Muslim at the
door of (your) chamber?' I say: 'Death as a Muslim at the door
of (my) chamber because I do not know whether (my) Islam
will remain as far as the door of the house or not.'" Abu Darda
used to swear: "No one is secure from having his faith taken
from him at the time of death."

Sahl Tustari says: "With every breath the truly righteous
are fearful of a bad ending." At the time of death Sufyan
Thawri, may God have mercy upon him, lamented and wept.
They said: "Do not weep, for the pardon of God Most High is
greater than your sins." He said: "If I knew I would die in the
Unity, I would not fear, even though I have sins in the amount
of several mountains." One of the saints made a will and gave
what things he had to a person, saying: "The sign of my dying
in (the faith of) the Unity (of God) is such-and-such a thing. If
you see that sign, buy sugar and almonds with that money
and toss them upon the children of the city and say: 'This is
the wedding of so-and-so who has escaped.' If you do not see
that sign say to the people of the city that they should not offer
a formal prayer for me and not be deceived by me so that after
death, anyway, I may not be a hypocrite."

Sahl Tustari says: "A disciple fears that he will fall into
sin, while the knower fears that he will fall into unbelief." Abu
Yazid says: "When I go to the mosque I see a belt about my
waist and until the moment I enter the mosque, I fear that it
will take me to a church. It is the same five times every day."
Jesus (ﷺ) said to his disciples: "You fear sins and we who are

prophets fear unbelief." One of the prophets was afflicted by much hunger, thirst, and trouble for many years. So he complained to God Most High and a revelation came: "I preserve thy heart from unbelief and thou art not delighted by that so that thou desirest the world?" He answered: "O Lord God, I repent and I have become delighted." He threw dust upon his head out of shame for his request.

One of the reasons for a bad ending is hypocrisy. It was for this that the Companions always were in fear of hypocrisy. Hasan Basri, may God have mercy upon him, said: "If I were sure that there is no hypocrisy in me, I would have no fear of anything on the face of the earth." And he said: "A difference between the inside and the outside and (between) the heart and the tongue is hypocrisy."

Know that the meaning of the bad ending of which all are afraid is that one's faith be taken away at the time of departure. There are many reasons for this and its knowledge is hidden, but it can be said in this book that it comes from two causes:

(1) One is that a person believes in a vain heresy and passes his life holding that (belief) and does not imagine that (the belief) itself could be a mistake. When death is near, affairs are revealed. It may be that that error be disclosed to him and for that reason he may become doubtful about the (other) beliefs that he had as well, because his confidence in his own belief has left him and he departs from the world holding those doubts. This peril is for the heretic and for the person who travels the path of scholastic dispute, even though he be pious. However the fools and the smug who are Muslims in appearance, as mentioned in the Quran and the Traditions, consider themselves secure from this. The Messenger (ﷺ) said about this: "Let the religion of old women be yours; most of the inhabitants of heaven are fools." For this reason the forefathers prohibited scholastic dispute, argument, and inquiry in

the essential nature of things, for they knew that not everyone can endure that and one quickly falls into heresy.

(2) The second reason is that (one's) faith is weak to begin with and the love for the world is victorious over the love for God Most High. At the time of death, when he sees that all his lusts are taken away from him and that he will be driven out of the world by force and be taken to a place he does not desire—perhaps because of the disliking of that which He does to him—he will change and the weak love (he formerly had for God) will also be nullified; as a person who loves a child, but that love is weak. When that child takes something which (the parent) loves more than he loves the child, he takes the child as an enemy and that amount of love which he had is also lost. It is for this that the rank of martyrdom is so great, for at that moment the world has departed from before him and the love for God has triumphed and he has laid his body on death. In such a state, death's arrival is a great booty, because this state changes rapidly and the heart will not continue in that character. So, for whomever the love of God Most High is stronger than all else, that will necessarily keep him from giving all of himself to the world. He is more secure from this danger. And when the moment of death arrives and he knows that the moment of seeing the Friend has come, the coming of death will not be displeasing and the love for God Most High will become triumphant. The love of the world becomes void and disappears. This is the sign of a good ending.

Therefore, whoever desires to distance himself from this peril must distance himself from heresy and believe in that which is in the Quran and the Traditions. He must strive so that God Most High becomes dominant over him and the love for the world becomes weak and vanishes. It weakens when one observes the limits of the Religious Law so that the world becomes loathsome to one and one averts oneself from it. The love for God Most High becomes stronger by always remembering Him and by association with His friends, not with the lovers of the world. So, if (your) love for the world be stronger, (your) affair is in (greater) danger, as He said in the Quran: "If you love your father, children, wife, property, ease, and all that you have more than God Most High, then be prepared until the command of God Most High arrives": *Then wait until God brings His command to pass.* (Q. 9:24)

(IV) THE WAY TO ACQUIRE FEAR (OF GOD)

Know that the first station of the stations of religion is certainty and gnosis (*marifat*). Then, fear arises from gnosis; and from fear asceticism, patience, and repentance arise. Truth, sincerity and care in the remembrance (of God) and continuous meditation appear from fear and from them familiarity and love arise, and this is the end of the stations. Satisfaction, commitment, and zeal: all of these follow upon love. As a consequence, the alchemy of (spiritual) happiness, after certainty and gnosis, is fear; whatever is after that cannot be managed without it. This may be obtained in three ways:

(1) The first way is through knowledge and gnosis; for when one has come to know oneself and God Most High, one will necessarily fear God Most High. Whoever has fallen into the claws of lion and who knows the (nature of the) lion will have no need for any treatment to become afraid; rather, he becomes fear itself! Whoever recognizes God Most High in His majesty and power, (Who is) without any need for mankind, and who recognizes himself in his helplessness and distress, sees himself truly in the claws of a lion. Moreover, anyone will necessarily be afraid who recognizes the decree of God Most High, that everything that will be until the Resurrection has been decreed—happiness for some without any means and hardship for others without any crime—instead, it is as He desires and that never changes. It is for this that the

Messenger (ﷺ) said: "Moses (ﷺ) argued with Adam (ﷺ) and Adam also argued with Moses. Moses said: 'God Most High brought you to Paradise and did so many good things; why did you disobey His command so that you threw yourself and us into affliction?' (Adam) answered: 'Was that sin preordained for me in the beginning?' (Moses) answered: 'Yes.' (Adam) said: 'Would I have been able to disobey His command?' (Moses) said: 'No.' So Adam overcame Moses. Moses was cut off by Adam and did not reply."

Many are the gates of gnosis which arise from fear; whoever is more insightful is more fearing, so that it is narrated: "Gabriel (ﷺ) and the Messenger (ﷺ) were both weeping. A revelation came to them: 'Why do ye weep when I have made you secure.' They said: 'O Lord God, we are not secure from Thy cunning.' He said: 'Remain in that manner.' It was from the perfection of their gnosis that they said: 'Let what He said to us—that we are safe—not be a test and that there be some mystery under that that we are unable to perceive.'" On the day (of the battle) of Badr, in the beginning the Muslim army had been weakened and the Messenger (ﷺ) was afraid. He said: "O Lord God, if these Muslims are destroyed on the face of the earth, no one will remain to worship Thee." (Abu Bakr) Siddiq said: "What oath do you swear by God Most High? He has promised you aid and He will necessarily execute His promise." The station of Siddiq at that moment was confidence in (God's) promise and generosity; while the station of the Messenger (ﷺ) was fear of cunning. This was more perfect because he knew that he could not perceive the secrets of Divine Affairs, His arrangements in the management of (His) kingdom, and the intention of His decree.

(2) The second way is that if one is unable (to achieve) gnosis, he should associate with those who fear (God) so that their fear may spread to him and he may distance himself from the heedless. By these means fear is obtained, although by imita-

tion, as a child's fear of snakes because he has seen his father flee from them. He too is afraid and runs away, even though he does not know the characteristics of snakes. This fear is weaker than the fear of one who knows, for if the child sees a few snake charmers who handle them, just as he fears by imitation, so he will feel safe by imitation and he touches them. One who knows the nature of snakes does not become secure about them. Therefore, one imitating the fear (of the knowers) must avoid associating with the complacent and heedless, especially that person who is outwardly learned.

(3) The third way is that when one cannot find such people with whom to associate—and there are few remaining in this era—one should listen to (stories of) their states and character and read of them in books. For this reason, we shall recount some of the states of the prophets and saints with respect to fear so that whoever has a modicum of intellect may know that they were the most intelligent, most insightful, and most virtuous of mankind, yet they feared thus. Others should be even more fearful.

(IV) STORIES OF MESSENGERS AND ANGELS

It is related that when Iblis was cursed (by God) Gabriel and Michael wept continuously. God Most High sent a revelation to them: "Why do ye weep?"—and He is More Knowing—they said: "O Lord God, We are not secure from Thy devisings." He said: "That is as it should be; be not complacent."

Muhammad bin al-Munkadir, may God be pleased with him, says: "When He created hell, the angels wept; when He created man, they became silent, for they knew that He had created it for them." The Messenger (ﷺ) says: "Gabriel never came to me but that a trembling fell upon me out of fear of God Most High." Anas says: "The Messenger (ﷺ) asked Gabriel: 'Why do I never see Michael smiling?' (Gabriel) answered: 'Since the Fire was created, he has not smiled.'"

Mujahid says: "David (ﷺ) wept for forty days with his head pressed against the ground until plants grew from his tears. A call came: 'O David, why dost thou weep?' (David) cried out: 'A stick would burn from the fire of my self.' Then God Most High accepted his repentance. (David) said: 'O Lord God, inscribe my sin upon the palm of my hand lest I forget it.' (God) complied. He would not extend his hand for any food or drink without seeing that and weeping. Sometimes he would be given a cup of water not full and he would fill that cup with his tears."

It is related that David (ﷺ) wept so much that he lost his strength. He said: "O Lord God, wilt Thou have mercy upon my weeping?" A revelation came: "Thou dost talk of weeping! Hast thou forgotten thy sin?" He answered: "O Lord God, how could I forget that when before my sin, when I recited the psalms, flowing water in the streams and the blowing wind in air would stop and the birds of the sky would gather over my head and the desert beasts would come to my place of prayer. Now there is nothing of that. O Lord God, what terror is this?" (God) said: "O David, that was the intimacy of devotion and this is the terror of sin. O David, Adam was my servant. I created him with My Own gracious hand and breathed My Own Spirit into him. I commanded the angels to prostrate themselves before him and I cloaked him with the honored robe of wonder. I placed the crown of dignity upon his head. He complained of his loneliness: I created Eve from his side and I brought them both to Paradise. I drove them out, despised and naked, from My Presence because of one sin. O David, listen! Listen to the truth: thou hadst Our devotion; We had thy devotion. I gave thee what didst desire. Thou didst commit a sin; We gave thee a reprieve. Now with all of this if thou dost turn back to Us, We shall accept thee."

Yahya bin Kathir says that there is a story that when David (ﷺ) was intent upon lamenting for his sin, he would not eat anything for seven days, nor go to his women. He would come to the desert and command Solomon (﷽) to call out: "O people of God, whoever desires to hear the lamentation of David, come." Then people from the towns, birds from their nests, wild animals and predatory beasts from the wildernesses, reptiles from the mountains and the desert would head for that place. He would begin with the praise of God Most High and the people would cry out. Then he would describe the features of heaven and hell. Then he would mourn his sin so that many people would die of fear and anxiety. Then Solomon (﷽) would stand over him and say: "Enough, O father, for many people have perished!" They would announce that so-and-so and so-and-so has received the command so that their family would come and carry off the corpses. Each person would pick up his corpse so that one day of the forty thousand people who were at the assembly thirty thousand had perished. He had two servant girls whose duty it was to seize him at the time of fear and hold him lest his limbs not come apart (from each other).

And John the son of Zechariah (﷽) used to worship in Jerusalem. He was a child. When (other) children called him to play (with them), he would say: "He has not created me for play." When he was fifteen, he went to the desert and left mankind. One day Zechariah (﷽) passed by him. He saw (his son) standing beside some water and was on the point of death from thirst. (John) was saying: "By Thy power, I will not drink water so long as I do not know what my place is with Thee." He had wept so much that no flesh remained upon his face and his teeth had become visible and he had placed a piece of felt on his face so that the people would not see it. There are many stories similar to these about the prophets.

(V) STORIES OF THE COMPANIONS AND THE FOREFATHERS

Know that when (Abu Bakr) Siddiq, with all of his greatness, would see a bird, he would say: "I wish that I were that bird." Abu Dharr Ghaffari would say: "I wish that I were a tree." Ayishah said: "I wish that there were neither name nor sign of me."

Sometimes Umar, when hearing a verse of the Quran, would fall down and become unconscious and people would visit him for several days. There would be something resembling two black lines on his face from weeping. He would say: "I wish that Umar had never been born of his mother." Once he was passing by a house. Someone was reciting the Quran. (The reciter) had come to the verse: *Lo! The doom of thy Lord will surely come to pass; there is none that can ward it off.* (Q. 53:7-8) He descended from his animal and threw himself against a wall out of weakness. They took him home and he was ill for a month and no one knew the cause of his illness.

When Ali bin al-Husayn, may God be pleased with him, would perform the obligatory purification (for formal prayer), his face would become pale. They would ask: "What is this?" He would say: "Do you not know before Whom I am about to stand?"

Musawwir bin Makhzamah could not endure listening to the Quran. One day a stranger who did not know (Musawwir's) custom, recited these verses: *On the Day when We shall gather the righteous unto the Beneficent, a goodly company, and drive the guilty into hell, herding;* (Q. 19:85-86) and said: "We are of the guilty, not of the pious." (Musawwir) said to him: "Recite it again." (The stranger) did so. (Musawwir) cried out and gave up the ghost.

Hatim Asamm says: "Do not be deceived by a fine place, for there is no place better than Paradise; do you know what happened to Adam in Paradise? Do not be deceived by a plethora of acts of worship; do you know what happened to Iblis? Do not be deceived by a lot of knowledge, for Balam Baur had reached the point in knowledge so that he knew the

Great Name of God Most High. Concerning him, it was revealed: *And his likeness is the likeness of the dog.* (Q. 7:176) And do not deceive yourself with looking upon good men, for relatives of the Messenger (ﷺ) saw him frequently and associated with him, but did not become Muslims.

Sari Saqati, may God have mercy upon him, says: "I look into my nose very day and ask if my face has become shamefaced." Ata-yi Sulami was one of the fearers. He did not laugh for forty years, nor did he look at the sky. He looked at the sky once and fell down out of fear. Every night he would pass his hand over himself several times to see whether he had been metamorphosed or not. When some calamity, trouble, or famine would reach the people, he would say: "All of this is because of my evil; if I were to die, the people would be delivered."

Ahmad Hanbal, may God have mercy upon him, says: "I offered supplications so that God Most High might open one of the doors of fear to me. He answered my supplications; I feared that I would lose my reason. I said: 'O Lord God, (let it be disclosed) according to one's ability to bear it.' Then my heart calmed down." One of the pious worshippers of God was seen weeping. He was asked: "Why do you weep?" He answered: "Out of fear of that Hour in which mankind will be summoned to present themselves at the Resurrection."

Someone asked Hasan Basri, may God have mercy upon him: "How are you?" He replied: "What would be the condition of a person who is with some people on the sea, the ship is wrecked and each one remains on a board?" They said: "Difficult." He said: "That is how I am." He also said: "It is related in the Traditions that one is brought out of hell after a thousand years. I wish that I could be that person." He said this because he feared the evil ending of eternal (damnation) in hell.

Umar (bin) Abd al-Aziz had a serving girl. One day she

woke up from sleep and said: "O Commander of the Believers, I dreamt something strange." He said: "Tell me." She said: "I saw hell burning. The bridge was stretched over it and the caliphs were brought out. First I saw Abd-al-Malik Marwan brought forth and told: 'Cross this bridge.' It was not long before he fell into hell. Then his son Walid bin Abd al-Malik was brought forth; he fell in at once. His son Sulayman bin Walid was brought forth and the same occurred." (Umar) said: "Continue." She said: "Then, O Commander of the Believers, they brought you forth." When she said that, Umar cried out, and fell down unconscious. The girl cried out: "By God, I saw that you had crossed safely!" The girl was crying out and he was writhing (on the floor).

Hasan Basri did not laugh for years; he would always appear like a tormented prisoner whose head is about to be cut off. He would be asked; "With all of your worship and striving, why are you so overtaken by troubles?" He would answer: "I am not certain that God Most High may not have seen something in me to make Him my enemy and say: 'Do whatever you wish, for I shall not have mercy upon you,' and all of my efforts will have been in vain."

There are many stories similar to these. Look, now, how they feared (God) and you feel secure! It is either because they had committed many sins and you have not, or because they had much gnosis, and you do not. You, by reason of foolishness and heedlessness, feel safe in spite of your many sins; and they, by reason of their clear perception and gnosis were anxious, in spite of their many acts of devotion.

3 [WHICH IS SUPERIOR, FEAR OR HOPE?]

At the same time that a person says there are many Traditions about the virtues of fear and hope, which of these two is superior and which should win over the other? Know that fear and hope are like two medicines. One does not say a medicine is superior, but that it is more beneficial. For fear and hope, as we have said about attributes, are deficient. The perfection of a human being is that he be immersed in his love for God Most High so that his remembrance takes hold of his totality and he does not think about the past or the ending themselves. Instead, he looks at time, but he does not look at time either, rather he looks at the Lord of time. When he pays attention to fear and hope, this becomes a veil; however, such a state is rare. So, whoever is approaching the time of death must be hopeful, for this increases love. And whoever is going from this world must be in the love of God Most High so that meeting Him will become his (spiritual) happiness, for there is pleasure meeting the Beloved.

But at other times, if a man is one of the heedless, fear must overwhelm him, because the triumph of hope would be a fatal poison for him. If he is pious and his states and conditions are free from vice, his fear and hope should be moderate and equal. When he is engaged in worship and devotions, hope should be stronger; for the purity of the heart in conversation with God is a kind of love. However, at the time of sinning, fear should be stronger. Indeed, during the time of doing lawful things, fear should predominate—if a man is worshipful. If not, he may fall into sin. Therefore, these are medicines the benefits of which change according to conditions and individuals. The answer to this (question) is not absolute.